JAPANESE NEWSPAPER COMPOUNDS

JAPANESE
NEWSPAPER
COMPOUNDS

The 1,000 Most Important in Order of Frequency

compiled by

TADASHI KIKUOKA

CHARLES E. TUTTLE COMPANY
Rutland, Vermont & Tokyo, Japan

Published by the Charles E. Tuttle Company, Inc.
of Rutland, Vermont & Tokyo, Japan
with editorial offices at
Suido 1-chome, 2-6, Bunkyo-ku, Tokyo

Library of Congress Catalog Card No. 76-125560
International Standard Book No. 0-8048-0919-4

First printing, 1970
Fifteenth printing, 1990

PRINTED IN JAPAN

◆ TABLE OF CONTENTS ◆

◆ PREFACE ◆

NEWSPAPERS play a vital role in everyday life—abroad, as well as at home. Developing the ability to read them in a foreign language is much too important to be left to chance; on the contrary, well-organized, graded study is essential. This book is presented to help the student of Japanese read newspapers accurately and attack strange words effectively. Its body is formed by a list of the most frequently used newspaper compounds, each formed by two characters, arranged in order of descending frequency. There is also a test, the answers to which are given on a separate page.

The compounds have been selected from the *Shimbun Yōgo-shū* 新聞用語集 (A Glossary of Journalistic Terms), Nihon Shimbun Kyokai, Tokyo, 1961, and the *Shimbungo-jiten* 新聞語辞典 (Dictionary of Journalistic Terms), Asahi Shimbun-sha, Tokyo, 1960. The original selection was made by Dr. Hiroshi Okubo at Hosei University, Tokyo, to help Japanese junior high school students, particularly seventh and eighth graders, read newspapers with greater understanding. The present list retains the original frequency of compounds. We recognize, however, that just as customs, attitudes, and institutions are subject to flux in this changing world, so words are subject to birth, maturity, death, and rebirth. A special effort was made, therefore, to replace obsolete words with more useful ones, while avoiding new words which have little possibility of survival.

The one thousand compounds presented in this book form the

active, core vocabulary which is necessary for newspaper reading. In order to master journalistic vocabulary, however, the study of this list should be coordinated with the actual reading of newspapers and periodicals. Furthermore, since many words unfold their meaning only in context, it is highly recommended that the student construct his own sentences while studying this list.

The test is designed to determine the student's general vocabulary and indicate his strengths and weaknesses. Five compounds are arranged into a set; each set is accompanied by six translations, five of which can be correctly matched with a compound. The sixth is intended to be close enough to the correct translation of one or more of the compounds to mislead the student who does not have a firm grasp of all compounds. The student must not only have the passive ability to match a compound with a correct translation, but he must also have the active ability to distinguish false approximations of meaning. Thus, there is a double difficulty to the test.

A compilation of this kind requires the cooperation and assistance of many people. A special word of appreciation goes to the graduate students at Seton Hall University who eagerly took part in the project and made use of every opportunity to master these compounds. Particular thanks should be expressed to Mr. Patrick Malloy for his untiring effort in calling my attention to errors.

To Dr. John B. Tsu, the director of the Institute of Far Eastern Studies, Seton Hall University, goes deep appreciation for his constant encouragement of this work. Without his understanding and support it would not have materialized.

TADASHI KIKUOKA
Seton Hall University

JAPANESE NEWSPAPER COMPOUNDS

◆ CHARACTER COMPOUNDS ◆

1	委 員	*iin*	committee member
2	問 題	*mondai*	problem, question
3	政 府	*seifu*	government, administration
4	組 合	*kumiai*	association, union
5	選 挙	*senkyo*	election
6	関 係	*kankei*	relation, connection
7	経 済	*keizai*	economy, finance
8	事 件	*jiken*	event, affair, incident
9	決 定	*kettei*	decision, determination
10	会 議	*kaigi*	meeting, conference, session
11	地 方	*chihō*	locality, district, region
12	調 査	*chōsa*	investigation, examination, inquiry
13	現 在	*genzai*	the present, up to now
14	社 会	*shakai*	society, public
15	労 働	*rōdō*	labor, toil
16	大 会	*taikai*	mass meeting, convention, rally
17	事 務	*jimu*	business, office work
18	民 主	*minshu*	democratic
19	会 社	*kaisha*	company, corporation
20	代 表	*daihyō*	representative, representation
21	計 画	*keikaku*	plan, scheme, program
22	発 表	*happyō*	announcement, publication

23	昨 年	*sakunen*	last year
24	学 校	*gakkō*	school
25	教 育	*kyōiku*	education
26	結 果	*kekka*	result, outcome, consequence
27	国 民	*kokumin*	a national, people
28	地 区	*chiku*	district, section
29	予 算	*yosan*	an estimate, budget
30	生 産	*seisan*	production, manufacture
31	午 後	*gogo*	afternoon, P.M.
32	工 場	*kōjō (kōba)*	factory, plant, mill
33	政 治	*seiji*	politics, government
34	運 動	*undō*	motion, exercise, movement
35	場 合	*baai*	an occasion, circumstances, case
36	生 徒	*seito*	a pupil
37	当 局	*tōkyoku*	the authorities
38	候 補	*kōho*	candidacy
39	支 部	*shibu*	branch, subdivision
40	共 産	*kyōsan*	communism (kyōsan-shugi 共産主義)
41	教 師	*kyōshi*	a teacher; *see* 60
42	必 要	*hitsuyō*	necessity, need, requirement
43	国 会	*kokkai*	the National Diet, a parliament, a congress
44	一 般	*ippan*	general, generally, ordinary
45	以 上	*ijō*	the above mentioned, more than
46	内 閣	*naikaku*	cabinet, (government) ministry
47	政 策	*seisaku*	policy
48	反 対	*hantai*	contrary, reverse, opposite
49	全 国	*zenkoku*	the whole country, national

50	記 事	*kiji*	a newspaper article
51	捜 査	*sōsa*	search, investigate (*same as* sōsaku 捜索)
52	予 定	*yotei*	prearrangement, schedule
53	資 金	*shikin*	funds, capital
54	中 央	*chūō*	central, center
55	時 間	*jikan*	time, hour
56	実 情	*jitsujō*	real condition, actual circumstances
57	対 抗	*taikō*	opposition, antagonism
58	届 出	*todokede*	report
59	監 督	*kantoku*	supervision, control, superintendence
60	教 諭	*kyōyu*	a teacher; *see* 41
61	協 議	*kyōgi*	conference, discussion
62	生 活	*seikatsu*	livelihood
63	方 針	*hōshin*	objective, plan
64	大 学	*daigaku*	university, college
65	整 理	*seiri*	putting in order, adjustment, regulation
66	長 官	*chōkan*	chief, (government) secretary
67	要 求	*yōkyū*	request, demand, requirement
68	本 部	*hombu*	headquarters
69	提 出	*teishutsu*	presentation, submit
70	対 策	*taisaku*	countermeasure
71	警 察	*keisatsu*	the police force, police station
72	違 反	*ihan*	violation, infringement
73	議 員	*giin*	member of the Diet, a congress, or a parliament

74	機 関	*kikan*	organ, mechanism, facilities
75	午 前	*gozen*	morning, A.M.
76	今 後	*kongo*	from now on, hereafter
77	割 当	*wariate*	allotment, quota
78	意 見	*iken*	opinion, view
79	研 究	*kenkyū*	research, study
80	事 業	*jigyō*	an enterprise
81	実 施	*jisshi*	enforcement, execution
82	投 票	*tōhyō*	voting, a poll
83	町 村	*chōson*	towns and villages
84	検 事	*kenji*	public prosecutor
85	新 聞	*shimbun*	newspaper, the press
86	管 理	*kanri*	management, control
87	業 者	*gyōsha*	businessman
88	一 部	*ichibu*	a part, portion
89	予 報	*yohō*	forecast, prediction
90	自 由	*jiyū*	freedom, liberty
91	主 義	*shugi*	-ism, principle; *see* 40
92	交 渉	*kōshō*	negotiations, discussions
93	高 校	*kōkō*	high school
94	援 助	*enjo*	assistance, aid
95	輸 出	*yushutsu*	export
96	態 度	*taido*	attitude, manner
97	行 政	*gyōsei*	administration
98	裁 判	*saiban*	a trial, judgment
99	改 正	*kaisei*	revision, alteration
100	中 心	*chūshin*	center, core
101	事 実	*jijitsu*	a fact, the truth
102	課 長	*kachō*	section chief

103	戸 主	*koshu*	the head of a household
104	責 任	*sekinin*	responsibility, duty
105	報 告	*hōkoku*	report, information
106	首 相	*shushō*	prime minister, premier
107	世 界	*sekai*	world
108	産 業	*sangyō*	industry
109	部 長	*buchō*	head of a section, department
110	特 別	*tokubetsu*	special, extraordinary
111	最 高	*saikō*	highest, supreme
112	子 供	*kodomo*	a child
113	学 生	*gakusei*	a student
114	企 業	*kigyō*	an enterprise, undertaking
115	価 格	*kakaku*	price, value
116	解 決	*kaiketsu*	settlement, solution
117	列 車	*ressha*	a train
118	取 調	*torishirabe*	investigation, examination
119	知 事	*chiji*	prefectural governor
120	最 近	*saikin*	the latest, most recent
121	協 力	*kyōryoku*	cooperation, collaboration
122	参 加	*sanka*	participation
123	食 糧	*shokuryō*	food, provisions, rations
124	賃 金	*chingin*	wages
125	以 来	*irai*	since, henceforth
126	農 業	*nōgyō*	agriculture
127	安 定	*antei*	stability, equilibrium
128	方 面	*hōmen*	direction, district
129	容 疑	*yōgi*	suspect, charge
130	貿 易	*bōeki*	foreign trade
131	検 挙	*kenkyo*	arrest, a roundup

132	指 導	*shidō*	leadership, guidance
133	引 揚	*hikiage*	repatriate
134	国 際	*kokusai*	international
135	相 当	*sōtō*	suitable, proper
136	県 下	*kenka*	under prefecture control, throughout prefecture
137	逮 捕	*taiho*	arrest, apprehension
138	共 同	*kyōdō*	cooperation, collaboration, joint
139	農 家	*nōka*	a farm family
140	程 度	*teido*	degree, grade, standard
141	希 望	*kibō*	hope, aspiration
142	政 党	*seitō*	political party
143	打 開	*dakai*	a break in the deadlock
144	一 方	*ippō*	one side, the other side
145	連 合	*rengō*	union, alliance
146	議 長	*gichō*	chairman
147	工 業	*kōgyō*	(manufacturing) industry
148	復 興	*fukkō*	revival, renaissance, reconstruction
149	会 長	*kaichō*	president, chairman
150	経 営	*keiei*	management, administration
151	総 裁	*sōsai*	president
152	決 勝	*kesshō*	decision of a contest
153	執 行	*shikkō*	enforcement, performance
154	年 度	*nendo*	year period
155	原 則	*gensoku*	principle
156	準 備	*jumbi*	preparation, arrangements
157	法 案	*hōan*	a bill (law)
158	解 散	*kaisan*	breakup, dissolution

159	検 討	*kentō*	an examination, investigation
160	取 引	*torihiki*	transactions, deal, business
161	局 長	*kyokuchō*	bureau director, office chief
162	職 員	*shokuin*	staff member, personnel
163	会 談	*kaidan*	conversation, conference
164	協 定	*kyōtei*	agreement, arrangement
165	措 置	*sochi*	a measure, step
166	銀 行	*ginkō*	a bank
167	臨 時	*rinji*	temporary, special, extraordinary
168	審 議	*shingi*	deliberation
169	理 由	*riyū*	reason, pretext, motive
170	記 者	*kisha*	a reporter
171	婦 人	*fujin*	woman, female
172	決 議	*ketsugi*	a resolution, decision
173	本 年	*honnen*	this (current) year
174	鉄 道	*tetsudō*	a railroad
175	発 見	*hakken*	a discovery
176	組 織	*soshiki*	organization, composition, anatomy, system
177	条 件	*jōken*	conditions, terms
178	外 相	*gaishō*	foreign minister
179	条 約	*jōyaku*	treaty, pact
180	理 事	*riji*	director, board of directors
181	農 林	*nōrin*	agriculture and forestry
182	金 融	*kin'yū*	monetary circulation, credit situation
183	建 設	*kensetsu*	construction, establishment
184	野 球	*yakyū*	baseball

185	闘 争	*tōsō*	strife, conflict
186	社 長	*shachō*	company president
187	運 営	*un'ei*	management, administration
188	国 家	*kokka*	state, nation
189	労 組	*rōkumi* (*rōso*)	labor union (rōdō-kumiai 労働組合)
190	議 会	*gikai*	the Diet, congress, parliament
191	取 締	*torishimari*	control, management, supervision
192	検 察	*kensatsu*	examination, prosecutor
193	模 様	*moyō*	pattern, figure, design
194	最 後	*saigo*	the last, end, conclusion
195	設 置	*setchi*	establishment, institution
196	協 会	*kyōkai*	association, organization, society
197	教 授	*kyōju*	teaching, instruction, professor
198	情 勢	*jōsei*	state of things, condition, situation
199	団 体	*dantai*	organization, association
200	公 務	*kōmu*	official business, public business
201	付 近	*fukin*	neighborhood, vicinity
202	平 均	*heikin*	an average
203	音 楽	*ongaku*	music
204	平 和	*heiwa*	peace, tranquillity
205	野 党	*yatō*	an opposition party
206	実 現	*jitsugen*	materialization, realization
207	主 張	*shuchō*	claim, request, opinion
208	成 績	*seiseki*	results, rating
209	農 地	*nōchi*	agricultural land
210	統 制	*tōsei*	regulation, control

211	以 下	*ika*	below, less than, as follows
212	演 説	*enzetsu*	speech, address
213	文 化	*bunka*	culture, civilization
214	物 価	*bukka*	prices of commodities
215	輸 入	*yunyū*	import, introduction
216	期 待	*kitai*	expectation, anticipation
217	国 務	*kokumu*	affairs of state
218	財 政	*zaisei*	economy, financial affairs
219	自 分	*jibun*	myself, oneself
220	開 始	*kaishi*	commencement, start
221	立 場	*tachiba*	a situation, position
222	鋼 鉄	*kōtetsu*	steel (*same as* tekkō 鉄鋼)
223	目 標	*mokuhyō*	mark, objective
224	姿 勢	*shisei*	an attitude, posture
225	結 局	*kekkyoku*	after all, eventually
226	活 動	*katsudō*	action, activity
227	一 応	*ichiō*	once, at least
228	制 度	*seido*	system, institution
229	中 学	*chūgaku*	middle school, junior high
230	汚 染	*osen*	pollution
231	戦 争	*sensō*	war
232	家 庭	*katei*	home, household
233	放 送	*hōsō*	broadcasting
234	見 込	*mikomi*	hope, prospect, expectation
235	会 見	*kaiken*	interview
236	農 民	*nōmin*	farmers, peasants
237	保 守	*hoshu*	conservative
238	官 僚	*kanryō*	a bureaucrat, bureaucracy
239	市 内	*shinai*	(within a) city

240	出 席	*shusseki*	attendance, presence
241	起 訴	*kiso*	prosecution, indictment
242	正 式	*seishiki*	due form, formality
243	物 資	*busshi*	goods, materials
244	影 響	*eikyō*	influence
245	今 回	*konkai*	now, this time (*same as* kondo 今度)
246	内 容	*naiyō*	contents, matter, substance
247	記 録	*kiroku*	a record, minutes
248	基 準	*kijun*	standard, basis
249	全 部	*zembu*	all, entire, the whole
250	増 加	*zōka*	an increase, addition
251	週 間	*shūkan*	week, weekly
252	役 所	*yakusho*	a government office
253	被 害	*higai*	damage
254	給 与	*kyūyo*	allowance, grant, supply
255	税 務	*zeimu*	taxation business
256	可 能	*kanō*	possibility
257	女 子	*joshi*	women
258	当 選	*tōsen*	be elected, win the prize
259	工 事	*kōji*	construction work
260	努 力	*doryoku*	great effort, exertion
261	連 絡	*renraku*	a junction, connection, coordination
262	公 団	*kōdan*	a public corporation
263	人 事	*jinji*	personnel affairs, human affairs
264	失 業	*shitsugyō*	unemployment
265	会 計	*kaikei*	an account, finance
266	連 盟	*remmei*	a league, union, alliance

267	意 味	*imi*	meaning, significance
268	既 報	*kihō*	previous report
269	当 事	*tōji*	the matter under concern
270	負 担	*futan*	burden, charge, responsibility
271	支 払	*shiharai*	payment
272	困 難	*konnan*	difficulty, distress
273	保 健	*hoken*	health, hygiene
274	再 建	*saiken*	rebuilding, reconstruction, rehabilitation
275	留 学	*ryūgaku*	studying abroad
276	承 認	*shōnin*	recognition, acknowledgment
277	成 立	*seiritsu*	coming into existence, establishment, completion
278	農 村	*nōson*	agricultural community, farm village, rural
279	役 員	*yakuin*	an officer, official, the staff
280	収 容	*shūyō*	accommodate, receive
281	審 査	*shinsa*	judging, inspection
282	非 常	*hijō*	an emergency, extraordinary, unusual, very
283	原 因	*gen'in*	cause, origin, source
284	代 議	*daigi*	representing others in a conference
285	声 明	*seimei*	a declaration, statement
286	新 制	*shinsei*	new system
287	融 資	*yūshi*	financing, a loan
288	青 年	*seinen*	a youth, young man
289	再 開	*saikai*	reopening, resumption
290	人 員	*jin'in*	number of persons, personnel

291	運 転	*unten*	operation, motion
292	事 情	*jijō*	circumstances, considerations, conditions
293	改 革	*kaikaku*	reform, reformation, innovation
294	従 来	*jūrai*	up to now, so far, traditional
295	注 目	*chūmoku*	notice, attention, observation
296	予 選	*yosen*	nomination, a primary, preliminary contest
297	同 盟	*dōmei*	an alliance, league, union
298	本 社	*honsha*	head office, main office
299	十 分	*jūbun*	fully, in full, sufficient, plenty
300	目 的	*mokuteki*	aim, objective, intention
301	技 術	*gijutsu*	an art, technique
302	不 足	*fusoku*	insufficiency, shortage, deficiency
303	憲 法	*kempō*	constitution
304	言 明	*gemmei*	a declaration, statement, assertion
305	自 治	*jichi*	self-government, autonomy
306	調 整	*chōsei*	regulation, adjustment
307	超 過	*chōka*	excess
308	具 体	*gutai*	concrete, tangible, materialize
309	水 産	*suisan*	marine products
310	各 地	*kakuchi*	every place, various places
311	競 技	*kyōgi*	a game, match, contest
312	映 画	*eiga*	a movie, film
313	総 統	*sōtō*	a president, generalissimo
314	所 得	*shotoku*	income
315	和 平	*wahei*	peace
316	科 学	*kagaku*	science

317	施 設	*shisetsu*	an institution, establishment, facility
318	指 令	*shirei*	orders, instructions, directive
319	送 検	*sōken*	*sending* the person accused *to* the *prosecutor; see* 755
320	総 会	*sōkai*	a general meeting
321	提 案	*teian*	a proposal, proposition
322	強 化	*kyōka*	strengthen, intensify, reinforce
323	弁 護	*bengo*	defense, pleading, advocacy
324	諸 国	*shokoku*	various countries
325	許 可	*kyoka*	permission, approval
326	直 接	*chokusetsu*	direct, immediate
327	試 合	*shiai*	a match, game, bout
328	大 体	*daitai*	general, substantially, outline
329	委 託	*itaku*	entrust (a person with something)
330	幹 部	*kambu*	(executive) staff
331	機 構	*kikō*	a mechanism, organization
332	使 用	*shiyō*	use, employment
333	部 分	*bubun*	a portion, section
334	主 権	*shuken*	sovereignty, supremacy
335	同 時	*dōji*	simultaneous, concurrent
336	犯 人	*hannin*	an offender, criminal
337	以 外	*igai*	with the exception of
338	支 持	*shiji*	support, maintenance
339	指 定	*shitei*	designation
340	出 張	*shutchō*	an official tour, business trip
341	少 年	*shōnen*	boys, juveniles
342	要 望	*yōbō*	demand for, request

343	利 用	*riyō*	use, utilization
344	出 納	*suitō*	cashier (suitō-gakari 出納係)
345	規 定	*kitei*	regulation, provisions
346	評 論	*hyōron*	criticism, critique
347	大 臣	*daijin*	cabinet minister
348	判 決	*hanketsu*	a judicial decision, judgment, sentence
349	代 理	*dairi*	representation, agency, proxy
350	地 域	*chiiki*	area, region
351	見 通	*mitōshi*	prospect, outlook, insight
352	家 族	*kazoku*	a family, members of a family
353	修 正	*shūsei*	amendment, revision
354	将 来	*shōrai*	future, prospects
355	住 宅	*jūtaku*	a residence
356	外 交	*gaikō*	diplomacy
357	定 員	*teiin*	capacity (people)
358	法 律	*hōritsu*	law
359	目 下	*mokka*	at present, now
360	結 成	*kessei*	formation
361	退 職	*taishoku*	retirement from office
362	開 催	*kaisai*	*holding* a meeting, *open* an exhibition
363	辞 職	*jishoku*	resignation
364	完 全	*kanzen*	perfection, completeness
365	行 為	*kōi*	an act, deed, conduct
366	公 判	*kōhan*	a public trial
367	促 進	*sokushin*	promotion, acceleration
368	漁 業	*gyogyō*	fishing (industry)
369	建 築	*kenchiku*	construction, architecture

370	自 動	*jidō*	self-motion, automatic
371	都 市	*toshi*	towns and cities, municipal, urban
372	文 部	*mombu*	Ministry of Education (mombu-shō 文部省)
373	地 元	*jimoto*	local
374	質 問	*shitsumon*	a question, inquiry
375	実 行	*jikkō*	practice, performance, execution, realization
376	勢 力	*seiryoku*	influence, power
377	制 限	*seigen*	restriction, restraint, limitation
378	訪 問	*hōmon*	a call, visit
379	可 決	*kaketsu*	approval, adoption, passage
380	行 使	*kōshi*	use, exercise
381	総 合	*sōgō*	synthesis, putting together
382	行 動	*kōdō*	action, conduct, mobilization
383	繊 維	*sen'i*	a fiber
384	値 上	*neage*	price raising
385	対 立	*tairitsu*	confrontation, opposition, antagonism
386	為 替	*kawase*	a money order, bill of exchange
387	合 理	*gōri*	rational
388	調 停	*chōtei*	arbitration, conciliation, mediation
389	出 身	*shusshin*	graduate from, come from
390	重 要	*jūyō*	important, momentous
391	拘 留	*kōryū*	detention, hold a person in custody (*same as* ryūchi 留置)
392	市 民	*shimin*	citizen

393	総 務	*sōmu*	general business (affairs), manager, director
394	国 内	*kokunai*	internal, domestic
395	関 心	*kanshin*	concern, interest
396	申 入	*mōshiire*	an offer, proposition
397	公 安	*kōan*	public safety
398	合 同	*gōdō*	combination, incorporation
399	処 理	*shori*	disposition, disposal, dealing
400	水 準	*suijun*	water level, level, standard
401	説 明	*setsumei*	an explanation, exposition
402	機 械	*kikai*	machine, mechanism
403	有 力	*yūryoku*	powerful, influential, prominent
404	統 一	*tōitsu*	unity, uniformity, unification
405	村 長	*sonchō*	a village headman
406	通 信	*tsūshin*	correspondence, communication, news
407	意 向	*ikō*	an intention, inclination
408	重 大	*jūdai*	important, weighty, serious
409	廃 止	*haishi*	abolition, repeal
410	部 落	*buraku*	a subunit of the village
411	大 蔵	*ōkura*	Ministry of Finance (ōkurashō 大蔵省)
412	不 正	*fusei*	injustice, unfairness
413	児 童	*jidō*	children
414	出 火	*shukka*	outbreak of fire
415	添 削	*tensaku*	correction
416	公 共	*kōkyō*	public service
417	要 請	*yōsei*	a claim, demand, request
418	多 数	*tasū*	a great number, majority

419	拒 否	*kyohi*	refusal, rejection, veto
420	緊 急	*kinkyū*	urgent, pressing
421	試 験	*shiken*	an examination, test
422	現 金	*genkin*	cash, ready money
423	合 計	*gōkei*	total
424	状 態	*jōtai*	condition, situation, circumstances
425	優 勝	*yūshō*	victory, championship
426	記 念	*kinen*	commemoration
427	追 加	*tsuika*	an addition, supplement, appendix
428	支 店	*shiten*	a branch store (office)
429	同 様	*dōyō*	identical, equal to
430	交 通	*kōtsū*	communication, transportation, intercourse
431	市 場	*shijō*	marketplace
432	商 工	*shōkō*	commerce and industry
433	徹 底	*tettei*	thoroughness, completeness
434	警 視	*keishi*	a police superintendent, metropolitan police
435	楽 団	*gakudan*	an orchestra, band
436	戦 後	*sengo*	after the war, postwar
437	傾 向	*keikō*	a tendency, trend, inclination
438	外 国	*gaikoku*	a foreign country
439	維 持	*iji*	maintenance, preservation
440	閣 議	*kakugi*	a cabinet meeting
441	書 記	*shoki*	a clerk, secretary
442	衣 類	*irui*	clothing
443	完 成	*kansei*	completion, perfection

444	両 日	*ryōjitsu*	both days
445	民 間	*minkan*	civilian
446	基 本	*kihon*	foundation, basis, standard
447	誤 解	*gokai*	misunderstanding
448	手 続	*tetsuzuki*	formalities, proceedings
449	販 売	*hambai*	sale
450	同 村	*dōson*	same village (dōchō 同町, dōshi 同市, etc.)
451	検 査	*kensa*	inspection, examination
452	発 生	*hassei*	outbreak, occurrence, origin
453	補 助	*hojo*	assistance, subsidiary aid
454	電 気	*denki*	electricity
455	県 内	*kennai*	within the prefecture
456	製 品	*seihin*	manufactured goods
457	専 門	*semmon*	a specialty, subject of study, expert
458	契 約	*keiyaku*	a contract, compact, agreement
459	発 行	*hakkō*	issue (publications)
460	考 慮	*kōryo*	consideration
461	人 民	*jimmin*	the people, the public
462	対 象	*taishō*	object (of worship, etc.), subject (of taxation, etc.)
463	全 焼	*zenshō*	burned down, entirely destroyed
464	診 療	*shinryō*	medical, clinic (shinryōjo 診療所)
465	校 長	*kōchō*	a principal, headmaster
466	作 業	*sagyō*	work, operation
467	争 議	*sōgi*	a dispute, quarrel, strike
468	防 衛	*bōei*	defense, protection, self-defense

469	現 場	*gemba*	the actual spot, the scene
470	市 長	*shichō*	a mayor
471	政 権	*seiken*	political power
472	懲 役	*chōeki*	penal servitude, imprisonment with hard labor
473	実 際	*jissai*	practical, actual condition, status quo
474	赤 字	*akaji*	a deficit, go in the red
475	見 解	*kenkai*	an opinion, point of view
476	確 認	*kakunin*	affirmation, confirmation
477	開 拓	*kaitaku*	reclamation (of wasteland), cultivation
478	最 低	*saitei*	lowest, minimum
479	結 論	*ketsuron*	a conclusion, concluding remarks
480	書 類	*shorui*	documents, official papers
481	職 場	*shokuba*	one's post, place of work
482	運 輸	*un'yu*	transportation
483	博 士	*hakase* (*hakushi*)	doctorate, Ph.D.
484	引 上	*hikiage*	pulling up, raising
485	確 立	*kakuritsu*	establishment
486	危 険	*kiken*	a danger, peril, hazard
487	懇 談	*kondan*	an informal talk
488	最 初	*saisho*	the beginning, outset
489	報 道	*hōdō*	information, a report
490	病 院	*byōin*	a hospital
491	回 答	*kaitō*	a reply, answer (*same as* henji 返事)
492	主 食	*shushoku*	the staple food

493	官 房	*kambō*	a government secretariat
494	厚 生	*kōsei*	public welfare, Welfare Ministry (kōseishō 厚生省)
495	無 職	*mushoku*	without an occupation
496	完 了	*kanryō*	completion, a conclusion
497	業 務	*gyōmu*	business, affairs, duties
498	補 給	*hokyū*	a supply, supplying, replenishment
499	両 氏	*ryōshi*	both persons
500	勤 務	*kimmu*	service, duty, work
501	仕 事	*shigoto*	work, job, occupation
502	時 期	*jiki*	time, season
503	証 人	*shōnin*	a witness
504	相 談	*sōdan*	consultation, conference
505	時 代	*jidai*	a period, epoch, era
506	重 点	*jūten*	an important point, lay stress on
507	正 午	*shōgo*	noon, mid-day
508	輸 送	*yusō*	transport, transportation
509	確 保	*kakuho*	guarantee, ensure, maintain
510	勧 告	*kankoku*	advice, counsel, remonstrance
511	死 体	*shitai*	a corpse
512	次 官	*jikan*	a vice-minister, undersecretary
513	出 場	*shutsujō*	appearance, participation
514	職 業	*shokugyō*	occupation, business
515	不 当	*futō*	injustice, unreasonable, unfair
516	閣 僚	*kakuryō*	cabinet ministers
517	投 手	*tōshu*	a (baseball) pitcher
518	被 告	*hikoku*	a defendant
519	期 間	*kikan*	a term, period

520	攻 撃	*kōgeki*	an attack, offensive, criticism, censure
521	場 所	*basho*	place, location
522	絶 対	*zettai*	absolute, unconditional
523	到 着	*tōchaku*	arrival
524	肥 料	*hiryō*	manure, fertilizer
525	不 明	*fumei*	unknown, obscurity
526	法 務	*hōmu*	judicial affairs, Ministry of Justice (hōmushō 法務省)
527	普 通	*futsū*	generally, ordinarily, usually
528	強 制	*kyōsei*	coercion, compulsion
529	資 本	*shihon*	funds, capital, capitalism (shihon-shugi; *see* 91)
530	電 力	*denryoku*	electric power
531	土 地	*tochi*	a plot of land, lot, soil
532	保 障	*hoshō*	guarantee, security
533	棄 権	*kiken*	abstain from voting, renunciation of a right
534	財 産	*zaisan*	property, fortune, assets
535	衆 議	*shūgi*	House of Representatives (shūgiin 衆議院)
536	全 体	*zentai*	the whole, entirety
537	防 止	*bōshi*	prevention, a check
538	解 雇	*kaiko*	discharge, dismissal
539	基 礎	*kiso*	foundation, basis
540	株 式	*kabushiki*	a stock (company)
541	大 使	*taishi*	an envoy, ambassador
542	根 本	*kompon*	the origin, source, foundation, root

543	不 良	*furyō*	badness, delinquent, inferiority
544	当 然	*tōzen*	naturally, as a matter of course
545	総 額	*sōgaku*	the sum total, total amount (*same as* sōkei 総計)
546	従 業	*jūgyō*	be employed
547	所 帯	*shotai*	a household, housekeeping
548	保 護	*hogo*	protection, shelter, guardianship
549	公 認	*kōnin*	official recognition, authorization
550	次 第	*shidai*	order, precedence, circumstances, gradually
551	所 長	*shochō*	a chief, head
552	人 口	*jinkō*	population
553	延 長	*enchō*	extension, elongation, prolongation
554	勤 労	*kinrō*	labor, exertion, diligent service
555	所 属	*shozoku*	attached to, belong to
556	証 拠	*shōko*	proof, evidence, testimony
557	連 立	*renritsu*	an alliance, coalition
558	申 込	*mōshikomi*	apply for, make an application
559	製 造	*seizō*	manufacture, production
560	買 収	*baishū*	buying, purchase, corruption, bribery
561	収 入	*shūnyū*	income, receipts, revenue
562	一 切	*issai*	all, everything, without exception
563	管 内	*kannai*	within the jurisdiction of
564	現 行	*genkō*	present, current, in operation
565	転 換	*tenkan*	convert, divert
566	倉 庫	*sōko*	a storehouse, warehouse

567	詐 欺	*sagi*	fraud, swindle
568	幹 事	*kanji*	an executive secretary
569	禁 止	*kinshi*	prohibition, ban
570	言 葉	*kotoba*	words, speech
571	市 会	*shikai*	a city council
572	税 金	*zeikin*	a tax, duty
573	空 気	*kūki*	air, atmosphere
574	設 定	*settei*	establishment, institution, creation
575	宣 伝	*senden*	propaganda, publicity, propagation
576	道 路	*dōro*	road, highway
577	発 足	*hassoku* (*hossoku*)	starting, inauguration
578	賠 償	*baishō*	reparations, indemnity, compensation
579	手 当	*teate*	an allowance, compensation
580	最 終	*saishū*	last, final, closing
581	開 会	*kaikai*	opening of a meeting
582	災 害	*saigai*	a calamity, disaster, misfortune
583	中 止	*chūshi*	suspension, stoppage
584	命 令	*meirei*	a command, order
585	利 益	*rieki*	profits, gains
586	個 人	*kojin*	an individual
587	事 態	*jitai*	situation, present state of affairs
588	消 防	*shōbō*	fire fighting, fire department
589	町 長	*chōchō*	a town headman
590	取 扱	*toriatsukai*	treatment, service, handling

591	折 衝	*sesshō*	negotiation
592	恒 久	*kōkyū*	permanent, perpetuity
593	変 更	*henkō*	change, alteration, modification, amendment
594	支 出	*shishutsu*	expenditures, expenses
595	解 釈	*kaishaku*	interpretation
596	協 同	*kyōdō*	cooperation, association
597	現 地	*genchi*	the actual place, local
598	郵 便	*yūbin*	mail, postal service
599	暴 力	*bōryoku*	violence
600	顧 問	*komon*	adviser, consultant
601	自 宅	*jitaku*	one's home, residence
602	水 害	*suigai*	water damage, flood disaster
603	改 善	*kaizen*	betterment, improvement, amelioration
604	注 意	*chūi*	attention, care, interest
605	任 命	*nimmei*	appointment
606	安 全	*anzen*	safety, security
607	現 状	*genjō*	the present condition, existing state, status quo
608	観 察	*kansatsu*	observation, survey
609	編 成	*hensei*	organization, formation
610	横 領	*ōryō*	usurpation, embezzlement, misappropriation
611	県 議	*kengi*	prefectural assembly
612	死 亡	*shibō*	death, mortality
613	樹 立	*juritsu*	establish, create
614	地 位	*chii*	social position, status
615	罰 金	*bakkin*	a fine, penalty

616	復旧	*fukkyū*	restoration, restitution (*same as* fukkō 復興)
617	加工	*kakō*	manufacturing, processing
618	刑事	*keiji*	a criminal case, (police) detective
619	短大	*tandai*	a junior college
620	町歩	*chōbu*	a hectare (2.471 acres)
621	妨害	*bōgai*	disturbance, obstruction, hindrance
622	旅館	*ryokan*	a hotel, inn
623	資格	*shikaku*	qualification, competency, eligibility
624	批判	*hihan*	criticism, judgment, comment
625	通告	*tsūkoku*	an announcement, notice
626	確実	*kakujitsu*	certainty, reliability, soundness
627	支配	*shihai*	rule, control, dominate
628	停止	*teishi*	suspension, interruption
629	自供	*jikyō*	confession
630	海外	*kaigai*	foreign, abroad, overseas
631	通貨	*tsūka*	currency
632	強力	*kyōryoku*	powerful, strong
633	講和	*kōwa*	peace, conclude peace
634	設備	*setsubi*	equipment, accommodations
635	段階	*dankai*	gradation, grade, stage
636	衛生	*eisei*	health, hygiene, sanitation
637	教団	*kyōdan*	a religious organization
638	収賄	*shūwai*	accepting bribes, corruption, graft
639	前後	*zengo*	before and after, throughout

640	電 話	*denwa*	telephone
641	西 欧	*seiō*	Western Europe
642	独 立	*dokuritsu*	independence, self-support
643	補 正	*hosei*	correction
644	混 乱	*konran*	confusion, disorder, mixed-up
645	大 衆	*taishū*	masses, general public
646	関 連	*kanren*	relation, connection
647	最 大	*saidai*	the greatest, largest, maximum
648	条 例	*jōrei*	regulations, rules, laws
649	適 用	*tekiyō*	adaptation, application
650	展 開	*tenkai*	development, progress, deployment
651	討 議	*tōgi*	debate, discussion
652	参 院	*san'in*	House of Councilors (sangiin 参議院)
653	常 任	*jōnin*	standing, regular, permanent
654	当 面	*tōmen*	urgent, pressing, impending
655	学 部	*gakubu*	department of a university
656	住 所	*jūsho*	address
657	性 格	*seikaku*	character
658	主 任	*shunin*	person in charge, responsible official
659	振 興	*shinkō*	promotion, encouragement
660	討 論	*tōron*	a debate, discussion
661	会 場	*kaijō*	assembly hall, meeting place
662	月 末	*getsumatsu*	the end of the month
663	積 極	*sekkyoku*	positive, progressive
664	温 泉	*onsen*	hot springs
665	観 光	*kankō*	sight-seeing

666	運 賃	*unchin*	shipping expenses, (passenger) fare
667	獲 得	*kakutoku*	acquisition, possession
668	所 有	*shoyū*	one's possessions
669	支 給	*shikyū*	payment, allowance
670	範 囲	*han'i*	scope, sphere, range
671	蔵 相	*zōshō*	Minister of Finance
672	預 金	*yokin*	a deposit, bank account
673	工 作	*kōsaku*	work, construction, handicraft, maneuvering
674	全 然	*zenzen*	wholly, entirely, completely (*same as* mattaku 全く)
675	全 面	*zemmen*	the whole surface, entire
676	治 安	*chian*	public order
677	団 地	*danchi*	multi-unit apartments
678	原 料	*genryō*	raw materials
679	新 設	*shinsetsu*	newly organized or established
680	通 過	*tsūka*	passing, passage
681	成 功	*seikō*	a success, hit
682	請 求	*seikyū*	claim, demand, application
683	設 立	*setsuritsu*	establishment, foundation, institution
684	貨 物	*kamotsu*	cargo, freight
685	期 限	*kigen*	a term, period
686	球 場	*kyūjō*	a baseball stadium (yakyūjō 野球場)
687	指 名	*shimei*	name, nominate, designate
688	資 料	*shiryō*	materials, data
689	精 神	*seishin*	soul, spirit, mind

690	開 発	*kaihatsu*	cultivation, exploitation, development
691	整 備	*seibi*	equip completely, consolidation
692	復 活	*fukkatsu*	revival, resurrection
693	推 薦	*suisen*	recommendation
694	相 手	*aite*	a companion, partner
695	解 除	*kaijo*	cancellation, release, rescission
696	警 官	*keikan*	a police officer
697	講 演	*kōen*	a lecture, address
698	集 団	*shūdan*	a group, body, collectively
699	施 行	*shikō*	enforcement, operation
700	政 界	*seikai*	political circles
701	依 然	*izen*	still, as yet, as before
702	交 換	*kōkan*	exchange, barter, reciprocation
703	能 率	*nōritsu*	efficiency
704	県 庁	*kenchō*	prefectural government (office)
705	向 上	*kōjō*	rise, improvement, elevation
706	政 令	*seirei*	a government ordinance
707	封 建	*hōken*	feudalistic, feudalism
708	公 園	*kōen*	a park, public garden
709	財 源	*zaigen*	source of revenue, financial resources
710	健 康	*kenkō*	health
711	機 会	*kikai*	opportunity, chance
712	資 材	*shizai*	materials, resources
713	地 帯	*chitai*	zone, region, belt
714	消 息	*shōsoku*	news, personal inquiry
715	心 配	*shimpai*	worry, uneasiness, anxiety
716	双 方	*sōhō*	both parties, both sides, mutual

717	犯 罪	*hanzai*	criminal offenses
718	判 明	*hammei*	become clear, be confirmed
719	課 税	*kazei*	taxation, assessment
720	出 荷	*shukka*	shipping, fowarding, outgoing freight
721	証 明	*shōmei*	proof, verification
722	政 局	*seikyoku*	the political situation (outlook)
723	全 員	*zen'in*	all the members
724	派 遣	*haken*	dispatch (a delegate)
725	強 盗	*gōtō*	a felon, (armed) robber
726	国 有	*kokuyū*	nationalization, state ownership
727	安 打	*anda*	a base hit (baseball)
728	解 放	*kaihō*	liberation, emancipation, release
729	自 転	*jiten*	self-rotation
730	効 果	*kōka*	effect, result, efficacy
731	写 真	*shashin*	a photograph
732	船 舶	*sempaku*	ships, vessels
733	窃 盗	*settō*	a burglar, theft, larceny
734	中 小	*chūshō*	medium and small, minor
735	連 邦	*rempō*	a federal state, union
736	外 務	*gaimu*	foreign affairs, Foreign Minister (gaimu-daijin 外務大臣)
737	決 意	*ketsui*	resolution, determination (*same as* kesshin 決心)
738	権 限	*kengen*	power, authority, jurisdiction
739	党 内	*tōnai*	within the (political) party
740	方 法	*hōhō*	a way, method, means
741	規 則	*kisoku*	rule, regulation
742	特 殊	*tokushu*	special, particular

743	費 用	*hiyō*	cost, expense
744	会 員	*kaiin*	membership, member of society
745	摘 発	*tekihatsu*	exposure, disclosure, unmasking
746	有 権	*yūken*	a voting right, franchiseholder
747	陸 上	*rikujō*	on land, shore
748	一 行	*ikkō*	a party, company, troupe
749	寄 付	*kifu*	contribution, donation, endowment
750	受 取	*uketori*	a receipt
751	追 及	*tsuikyū*	thorough investigation, cross-examination
752	撤 廃	*teppai*	abolition, removal
753	就 任	*shūnin*	assumption of office, inauguration, installation
754	証 券	*shōken*	securities, bonds
755	身 柄	*migara*	sending the *person* accused to prosecutor; *see* 319
756	総 長	*sōchō*	(university) president, (U.N.) secretary-general
757	滞 納	*tainō*	nonpayment, delinquent in payment
758	立 会	*tachiai*	attendance, presence, witnessing
759	以 内	*inai*	within, less than, not exceeding
760	観 測	*kansoku*	observation
761	自 殺	*jisatsu*	suicide
762	中 立	*chūritsu*	neutrality
763	土 木	*doboku*	civil engineering, public works
764	表 彰	*hyōshō*	commendation, award
765	集 中	*shūchū*	concentration, centralize

766	押 収	*ōshū*	confiscation, forfeiture (*same as* bosshū 没収)
767	自 身	*jishin*	myself, personal
768	底 値	*sokone*	the bottom price
769	国 立	*kokuritsu*	national, state
770	延 期	*enki*	postponement, adjournment
771	健 全	*kenzen*	healthy, wholesome, sound
772	通 知	*tsūchi*	report, notice, inform
773	役 場	*yakuba*	a village office (mura-yakuba 村役場)
774	了 解	*ryōkai*	understanding, comprehension
775	給 料	*kyūryō*	pay, wages, salary
776	自 立	*jiritsu*	independence, self-support
777	互 選	*gosen*	mutual election
778	消 極	*shōkyoku*	negative
779	中 旬	*chūjun*	middle ten days of the month
780	人 気	*ninki*	popularity
781	発 言	*hatsugen*	utterance, proposal
782	半 分	*hambun*	half
783	不 安	*fuan*	uneasiness, unrest, anxiety
784	事 前	*jizen*	beforehand
785	公 約	*kōyaku*	a public promise
786	辞 表	*jihyō*	letter of resignation
87	世 話	*sewa*	aid, care, assistance
788	定 期	*teiki*	fixed, regular, periodical
789	分 会	*bunkai*	a branch, chapter
790	国 庫	*kokko*	the national treasury
791	衆 院	*shūin*	House of Representatives
792	地 主	*jinushi*	a landlord, landowner

793	化 学	*kagaku*	chemistry
794	過 去	*kako*	the past, bygone days
795	大 幅	*ōhaba*	a full width, big scale
796	本 道	*hondō*	the main road, highway
797	更 迭	*kōtetsu*	a change, shake-up
798	信 任	*shinnin*	trust, confidence
799	始 末	*shimatsu*	disposition, settlement, management
800	単 位	*tan'i*	a unit, (school) credit
801	人 間	*ningen*	human beings
802	閉 鎖	*heisa*	closing, closure, lockout
803	署 名	*shomei*	a signature
804	数 名	*sūmei*	a few people
805	打 合	*uchiawase*	arrangement, consultation
806	適 当	*tekitō*	suitable, proper, adequate
807	府 県	*fuken*	prefectures
808	面 積	*menseki*	area, dimensions
809	木 材	*mokuzai*	wood, timber (*same as* zaimoku 材木)
810	告 発	*kokuhatsu*	prosecution, indictment, charge
811	削 減	*sakugen*	cut, reduction, curtailment
812	指 示	*shiji*	indication, directions, instructions
813	実 力	*jitsuryoku*	merit, real ability, efficiency
814	募 集	*boshū*	recruiting
815	完 納	*kannō*	pay in full
816	強 調	*kyōchō*	stress, emphasis
817	採 用	*saiyō*	adoption, employ
818	次 長	*jichō*	a vice-chief, vice-director
819	数 字	*sūji*	a figure, numeral

820	人 物	*jimbutsu*	a person, talented man
821	配 置	*haichi*	arrangement, disposition
822	払 下	*haraisage*	sell, disposition
823	労 務	*rōmu*	manual labor
824	応 援	*ōen*	aid, reinforcement, rescue, backing
825	終 了	*shūryō*	end, close, conclusion (*same as* owari 終り)
826	台 風	*taifū*	a typhoon
827	陳 情	*chinjō*	petition, appeal
828	逃 走	*tōsō*	an escape, flight, desertion
829	否 定	*hitei*	denial, negation, disavowal
830	封 鎖	*fūsa*	a blockade
831	分 裂	*bunretsu*	a split, disunion, disruption, fission
832	無 理	*muri*	unreasonable, unjust, unnatural
833	会 期	*kaiki*	a session, term
834	気 持	*kimochi*	a feeling, sensation, mood
835	公 民	*kōmin*	a citizen
836	通 商	*tsūshō*	trade and commerce
837	両 名	*ryōmei*	both persons
838	営 業	*eigyō*	a business, trade
839	自 然	*shizen*	nature
840	小 作	*kosaku*	tenancy
841	中 間	*chūkan*	the middle, midway
842	互 恵	*gokei*	reciprocal, reciprocity
843	共 和	*kyōwa*	a republic (kyōwa-koku 共和国)
844	新 人	*shinjin*	a new face, new star
845	代 金	*daikin*	a price

846	両 国	*ryōkoku*	both countries
847	引 続	*hikitsuzuki*	continually, continue doing
848	実 質	*jisshitsu*	substance, essence, quality
849	収 穫	*shūkaku*	harvest, crop, yield
850	卒 業	*sotsugyō*	graduation
851	原 告	*genkoku*	a plaintiff
852	回 復	*kaifuku*	revival, restoration, recovery
853	講 堂	*kōdō*	a lecture hall, auditorium
854	主 要	*shuyō*	chief, leading, principal
855	態 勢	*taisei*	attitude, arrangements
856	皇 居	*kōkyo*	the Imperial Palace (*same as* kyūjō 宮城)
857	一 時	*ichiji*	a time, temporarily, at one time
858	官 庁	*kanchō*	government offices
859	左 派	*saha*	the left wing, leftists
860	支 局	*shikyoku*	a branch office
861	手 配	*tehai*	arrangements, preparations
862	進 出	*shinshutsu*	advance, march, expansion
863	達 成	*tassei*	culmination, achievement, attainment (*same as* tassuru 達する)
864	担 当	*tantō*	in charge of
865	飛 行	*hikō*	a flight, aviation
866	犠 牲	*gisei*	a sacrifice, victim, offering
867	権 利	*kenri*	a right, claim, privilege
868	公 開	*kōkai*	open to the public
869	小 学	*shōgaku*	elementary (school)
870	申 告	*shinkoku*	report, statement, filling a form
871	前 回	*zenkai*	the last time, last session
872	単 一	*tan'itsu*	singleness, simplicity

873	気 象	*kishō*	the weather, atmospheric phenomena
874	警 戒	*keikai*	watch, lookout, vigilance
875	組 閣	*sokaku*	organize a new cabinet
876	大 量	*tairyō*	a large quantity
877	上 程	*jōtei*	introduce, present a bill (in parliament)
878	損 害	*songai*	a damage, loss
879	体 育	*taiiku*	physical education
880	提 供	*teikyō*	an offer, provide
881	人 権	*jinken*	human rights
882	判 事	*hanji*	a judge
883	無 視	*mushi*	ignore, disregard
884	県 民	*kemmin*	prefectural inhabitants
885	失 敗	*shippai*	a failure
886	追 放	*tsuihō*	a purge, banishment, exile, get rid of
887	累 増	*ruizō*	continuous increase
888	現 実	*genjitsu*	reality, actuality, realities of life
889	減 少	*genshō*	a decrease, diminution
890	拡 大	*kakudai*	magnify, enlarge
891	耕 地	*kōchi*	arable land, farm land
892	出 頭	*shuttō*	appearance, presence
893	練 習	*renshū*	training, practice, drill
894	金 額	*kingaku*	a sum of money
895	指 揮	*shiki*	a command, order, instruction
896	将 軍	*shōgun*	a general, shogun
897	美 術	*bijutsu*	the fine arts
898	表 明	*hyōmei*	an expression, manifestation

899	物 語	*monogatari*	a tale, story, narrative
900	解 説	*kaisetsu*	an explanation, commentary
901	経 費	*keihi*	expenses, cost, disbursement
902	告 示	*kokuji*	notification, announcement
903	就 職	*shūshoku*	finding employment
904	能 力	*nōryoku*	an ability, capacity
905	発 電	*hatsuden*	generation of electricity
906	暴 行	*bōkō*	a violence, outrage
907	街 頭	*gaitō*	a street
908	危 機	*kiki*	a crisis, critical moment
909	全 般	*zempan*	the whole
910	会 館	*kaikan*	a hall, assembly hall
911	限 度	*gendo*	a limit, limitation
912	手 段	*shudan*	a means, way, steps
913	趣 旨	*shushi*	meaning, gist (*same as* yōshi 要旨)
914	出 発	*shuppatsu*	a start, departure
915	税 制	*zeisei*	a tax system
916	中 継	*chūkei*	relay
917	各 種	*kakushu*	every kind, various kinds
918	行 方	*yukue*	whereabouts
919	院 長	*inchō*	director, principal
920	携 帯	*keitai*	carry, bring, portable
921	鉱 山	*kōzan*	a mine
922	商 業	*shōgyō*	a trade, commerce
923	慎 重	*shinchō*	careful, cautious, discretion
924	推 定	*suitei*	presumption, inference, estimation
925	戦 前	*senzen*	prewar
926	突 破	*toppa*	break through, overcome, pass

927	内 部	*naibu*	the interior, inside
928	発 展	*hatten*	development, growth, expansion
929	鉱 業	*kōgyō*	mining industry
930	司 会	*shikai*	presiding, chairmanship
931	師 範	*shihan*	a master, instructor, teacher
932	派 閥	*habatsu*	factionalism
933	宣 言	*sengen*	declaration, proclamation
934	長 期	*chōki*	a long term, long period
935	統 計	*tōkei*	statistics
936	競 争	*kyōsō*	a contest, competition
937	製 作	*seisaku*	manufacturing, production
938	首 班	*shuhan*	the head position
939	諮 問	*shimon*	an inquiry, investigation
940	納 税	*nōzei*	payment of taxes
941	方 式	*hōshiki*	a formula, method, form
942	循 環	*junkan*	circulation, rotation, cycle
943	首 脳	*shunō*	the brains, leaders
944	耕 作	*kōsaku*	cultivation, farming
945	奨 励	*shōrei*	encouragement, give impetus to
946	途 中	*tochū*	on the way, en route
947	法 廷	*hōtei*	court of law
948	野 菜	*yasai*	vegetables
949	養 蚕	*yōsan*	sericulture
950	援 護	*engo*	backing, support, protection
951	高 等	*kōtō*	high-grade, advanced
952	思 想	*shisō*	thought, idea, concept
953	放 棄	*hōki*	abandonment, renunciation
954	約 束	*yakusoku*	a promise, engagement, appointment

955	話 合	*hanashiai*	conference, consultation
956	義 務	*gimu*	obligation, responsibility, duty
957	求 刑	*kyūkei*	prosecution
958	経 験	*keiken*	experience
959	出 版	*shuppan*	publication
960	処 置	*shochi*	a measure, action, disposition, dealing
961	核 爆	*kakubaku*	nuclear explosion (kakubaku-hatsu 核爆発)
962	相 場	*sōba*	market price, speculation
963	海 上	*kaijō*	the sea, maritime
964	打 切	*uchikiri*	the end, close, finish
965	支 所	*shisho*	a branch office, substation
966	直 後	*chokugo*	immediately after
967	投 資	*tōshi*	investment
968	経 過	*keika*	progression, development, course
969	除 名	*jomei*	expulsion, be expelled
970	信 用	*shin'yō*	credit, confidence, trust
971	夕 刻	*yūkoku*	in the evening, dusk (*same as* yūgata 夕方)
972	総 理	*sōri*	prime minister, premier
973	変 化	*henka*	a change, variation, variety
974	活 発	*kappatsu*	active, liveliness, briskness
975	項 目	*kōmoku*	a heading, item, article, paragraph
976	織 物	*orimono*	textiles
977	党 員	*tōin*	a party member
978	前 期	*zenki*	the first term, first half year
979	文 学	*bungaku*	literature

980	法 規	*hōki*	law
981	指 摘	*shiteki*	indicate, point out
982	署 長	*shochō*	a police chief, tax director
983	賛 成	*sansei*	approve, agree, be in favor of
984	処 分	*shobun*	disposal, punishment
985	聴 取	*chōshu*	listening, hearing
986	衛 星	*eisei*	a satellite
987	矛 盾	*mujun*	contradiction
988	入 札	*nyūsatsu*	submit a bid
989	陪 審	*baishin*	jury
990	外 貨	*gaika*	foreign currency
991	娯 楽	*goraku*	amusement, entertainment
992	景 気	*keiki*	an (economic) boom
993	伝 道	*dendō*	missionary work
994	伝 染	*densen*	be infected, spread
995	障 壁	*shōheki*	a barrier, obstacle (*same as* shōgai 障害)
996	加 盟	*kamei*	alliance, entry
997	忙 殺	*bōsatsu*	be busily occupied
998	借 款	*shakkan*	a loan
999	提 携	*teikei*	cooperation, coalition
1000	締 結	*teiketsu*	conclusion, conclude a treaty

◆ TEST ◆

1. 組 合	a. rally	21. 捜 査	a. funds
2. 選 挙	b. labor	22. 資 金	b. supervision
3. 調 査	c. inquiry	23. 監 督	c. objective
4. 労 働	d. election	24. 方 針	d. put in order
5. 大 会	e. democratic	25. 整 理	e. search
	f. union		f. countermeasure

6. 事 務	a. plan	26. 要 求	a. police
7. 代 表	b. announcement	27. 提 出	b. violation
8. 計 画	c. education	28. 警 察	c. request
9. 発 表	d. locality	29. 違 反	d. organ
10. 教 育	e. representation	30. 機 関	e. chief
	f. office work		f. submit

11. 結 果	a. politics	31. 割 当	a. opinion
12. 予 算	b. in case	32. 意 見	b. prosecutor
13. 政 治	c. pupil	33. 検 事	c. quota
14. 場 合	d. national	34. 管 理	d. management
15. 生 徒	e. budget	35. 予 報	e. forecast
	f. result		f. enterprise

16. 当 局	a. need	36. 主 義	a. trial
17. 候 補	b. cabinet	37. 援 助	b. export
18. 必 要	c. policy	38. 輸 出	c. -ism
19. 内 閣	d. government	39. 裁 判	d. assistance
20. 政 策	e. candidacy	40. 改 正	e. revision
	f. authorities		f. administration

41.	課 長	a.	report
42.	報 告	b.	highest
43.	産 業	c.	enterprise
44.	最 高	d.	section chief
45.	企 業	e.	extraordinary
		f.	industry

46.	最 近	a.	cooperation
47.	協 力	b.	food
48.	食 糧	c.	most recent
49.	賃 金	d.	since
50.	以 来	e.	participation
		f.	wages

51.	安 定	a.	suspect
52.	容 疑	b.	leadership
53.	貿 易	c.	stability
54.	指 導	d.	international
55.	国 際	e.	management
		f.	foreign trade

56.	逮 捕	a.	degree
57.	程 度	b.	break
58.	打 開	c.	arrest
59.	連 合	d.	reconstruction
60.	復 興	e.	cooperation
		f.	alliance

61.	総 裁	a.	jurisdiction
62.	執 行	b.	transaction
63.	原 則	c.	dissolution
64.	解 散	d.	president
65.	取 引	e.	principle
		f.	enforcement

66.	協 定	a.	railroad
67.	臨 時	b.	agreement
68.	審 議	c.	preparation
69.	決 議	d.	temporary
70.	鉄 道	e.	deliberation
		f.	resolution

71.	組 織	a.	terms
72.	条 件	b.	treaty
73.	条 約	c.	conflict
74.	金 融	d.	construction
75.	闘 争	e.	organization
		f.	monetary circulation

76.	運 営	a.	control
77.	労 組	b.	pattern
78.	取 締	c.	establishment
79.	模 様	d.	association
80.	団 体	e.	management
		f.	labor union

81.	平 均	a.	rating
82.	実 現	b.	speech
83.	成 績	c.	average
84.	演 説	d.	peace
85.	物 価	e.	materialization
		f.	prices of commodities

86.	輸 入	a.	objective
87.	財 政	b.	position
88.	立 場	c.	import
89.	目 標	d.	posture
90.	姿 勢	e.	request
		f.	financial affairs

91.	活 動	a.	attendance
92.	汚 染	b.	activity
93.	保 守	c.	bureaucrat
94.	官 僚	d.	conservative
95.	出 席	e.	system
		f.	pollution

96.	正 式	a.	record
97.	物 資	b.	influence
98.	影 響	c.	formality
99.	記 録	d.	goods
100.	基 準	e.	basis
		f.	expectation

101.	被 害	a.	liaison
102.	税 務	b.	grant
103.	当 選	c.	damage
104.	連 絡	d.	corporation
105.	公 団	e.	taxation
		f.	elected

106.	失 業	a.	alliance
107.	負 担	b.	payment
108.	支 払	c.	burden
109.	保 健	d.	health
110.	連 盟	e.	construction
		f.	unemployment

111.	承 認	a.	cause
112.	農 村	b.	recognition
113.	収 容	c.	statement
114.	原 因	d.	accommodate
115.	声 明	e.	emergency
		f.	farm village

116.	融 資	a.	new system
117.	再 開	b.	up to now
118.	運 転	c.	financing
119.	改 革	d.	reopening
120.	従 来	e.	operation
		f.	reform

121.	不 足	a.	excess
122.	超 過	b.	shortage
123.	映 画	c.	concrete
124.	所 得	d.	movie
125.	具 体	e.	income
		f.	adjustment

126.	科 学	a.	facility
127.	施 設	b.	proposal
128.	提 案	c.	science
129.	弁 護	d.	defense
130.	許 可	e.	approval
		f.	reinforce

131.	委 託	a.	support
132.	犯 人	b.	section
133.	支 持	c.	entrust
134.	指 定	d.	offender
135.	要 望	e.	designation
		f.	request

136.	利 用	a.	sentence
137.	規 定	b.	area
138.	大 臣	c.	utilization
139.	判 決	d.	representation
140.	地 域	e.	regulation
		f.	cabinet minister

141.	見 通	a.	capacity
142.	修 正	b.	at present
143.	住 宅	c.	prospect
		d.	revision
144.	目 下	e.	residence
145.	辞 職	f.	resignation

146.	行 為	a.	local
147.	促 進	b.	automatic
		c.	conduct
148.	自 動	d.	practice
149.	地 元	e.	formation
150.	実 行	f.	acceleration

151.	制 限	a.	execution
152.	可 決	b.	rational
		c.	fiber
153.	行 使	d.	restriction
154.	繊 維	e.	approval
155.	合 理	f.	arbitration

156.	重 要	a.	offer
157.	申 入	b.	level
		c.	public safety
158.	公 安	d.	detention
159.	処 理	e.	disposal
160.	水 準	f.	important

161.	説 明	a.	intention
162.	通 信	b.	powerful
		c.	abolition
163.	意 向	d.	injustice
164.	廃 止	e.	communication
165.	不 正	f.	explanation

166.	児 童	a.	cash
167.	現 金	b.	refusal
		c.	condition
168.	要 請	d.	money order
169.	拒 否	e.	request
170.	状 態	f.	grade children

171.	記 念	a.	branch
172.	支 店	b.	market
		c.	city
173.	交 通	d.	transportation
174.	市 場	e.	commemoration
175.	戦 後	f.	postwar

176.	傾 向	a.	clerk
177.	書 記	b.	sale
		c.	civil
178.	完 成	d.	tendency
179.	民 間	e.	foundation
180.	販 売	f.	completion

181.	専 門	a.	issue
182.	契 約	b.	outbreak
		c.	clinic
183.	発 行	d.	contract
184.	考 慮	e.	specialty
185.	診 療	f.	consideration

186.	争 議	a.	view
187.	防 衛	b.	dispute
		c.	deficit
188.	懲 役	d.	defense
189.	赤 字	e.	operation
190.	見 解	f.	penal servitude

191.	開 拓	a.	place of work
192.	最 低	b.	establishment
193.	結 論	c.	reclamation
194.	書 類	d.	minimum
195.	職 場	e.	conclusion
		f.	documents

216.	解 雇	a.	discharge
217.	基 礎	b.	be employed
218.	従 業	c.	world unity
219.	公 認	d.	foundation
220.	所 帯	e.	a household
		f.	authorization

196.	報 道	a.	supply
197.	病 院	b.	report
198.	厚 生	c.	hospital
199.	完 了	d.	welfare
200.	補 給	e.	answer
		f.	completion

221.	人 口	a.	bribery
222.	連 立	b.	evidence
223.	収 入	c.	income
224.	証 拠	d.	purchase
225.	買 収	e.	a coalition
		f.	population

201.	証 人	a.	transportation
202.	相 談	b.	counsel
203.	時 代	c.	a period
204.	勧 告	d.	a witness
205.	輸 送	e.	export
		f.	consultation

226.	詐 欺	a.	publicity
227.	禁 止	b.	a tax
228.	市 会	c.	prohibition
229.	税 金	d.	fraud
230.	宣 伝	e.	information
		f.	a city council

206.	職 業	a.	occupation
207.	閣 僚	b.	cabinet ministers
208.	被 告	c.	pavilion
209.	不 明	d.	arrival
210.	到 着	e.	a defendant
		f.	unknown

231.	賠 償	a.	reparations
232.	災 害	b.	profits
233.	利 益	c.	a disaster
234.	事 態	d.	situation
235.	命 令	e.	a command
		f.	fire damage

211.	普 通	a.	regulation
212.	強 制	b.	capital
213.	棄 権	c.	abstain from voting
214.	法 務	d.	ordinarily
215.	資 本	e.	compulsion
		f.	judicial affairs

236.	恒 久	a.	negotiation
237.	折 衝	b.	collision
238.	解 釈	c.	interpretation
239.	郵 便	d.	permanent
240.	暴 力	e.	mail
		f.	violence

241.	改 善	a.	appointment
242.	安 全	b.	improvement
243.	現 状	c.	status quo
		d.	security
244.	死 亡	e.	life
245.	任 命	f.	death

246.	罰 金	a.	judgment
247.	復 旧	b.	criticism
248.	妨 害	c.	a notice
		d.	hindrance
249.	通 告	e.	a fine
250.	批 判	f.	restoration

251.	確 実	a.	reliability
252.	支 配	b.	rule
253.	海 外	c.	equipment
		d.	overseas
254.	設 備	e.	currency
255.	通 貨	f.	establishment

256.	独 立	a.	adaptation
257.	混 乱	b.	independence
258.	適 用	c.	development
		d.	confusion
259.	展 開	e.	dependence
260.	衛 生	f.	hygiene

261.	討 議	a.	promotion
262.	振 興	b.	character
263.	性 格	c.	acquisition
		d.	attack
264.	獲 得	e.	discussion
265.	常 任	f.	regular

266.	支 給	a.	model pattern
267.	範 囲	b.	sight-seeing
268.	預 金	c.	a deposit
		d.	entire
269.	全 面	e.	provision
270.	観 光	f.	sphere

271.	団 地	a.	nominate
272.	治 安	b.	administration
		c.	multi-unit
273.	期 限		apartments
274.	請 求	d.	public order
		e.	a period
275.	指 名	f.	claim

276.	復 活	a.	revival
277.	推 薦	b.	recommenda- tion
278.	警 官	c.	exploitation
		d.	a police officer
279.	政 界	e.	political circles
280.	開 発	f.	departure

281.	交 換	a.	construction
282.	能 率	b.	financial resources
283.	向 上	c.	elevation
		d.	exchange
284.	封 建	e.	efficiency
285.	財 源	f.	feudalism

286.	地 帯	a.	zone
287.	消 息	b.	offenses
		c.	personal inquiry
288.	犯 罪	d.	political situa- tion
289.	政 局	e.	taxation
290.	課 税	f.	govt. bureau

291.	解 放	a.	effect
292.	外 務	b.	foreign affairs
293.	効 果	c.	emancipation
294.	窃 盗	d.	a burglar
295.	国 有	e.	dissolve
		f.	nationalization

296.	権 限	a.	jurisdiction
297.	党 内	b.	disclosure
298.	寄 付	c.	donation
299.	摘 発	d.	within the party
300.	規 則	e.	departure
		f.	regulation

301.	就 任	a.	mediation
302.	証 券	b.	abolition
303.	撤 廃	c.	inauguration
304.	中 立	d.	bonds
305.	追 及	e.	thorough investigation
		f.	neutrality

306.	集 中	a.	concentration
307.	底 値	b.	measurement
308.	延 期	c.	the bottom price
309.	押 収	d.	postponement
310.	観 測	e.	observation
		f.	confiscation

311.	不 安	a.	uneasiness
312.	公 約	b.	negative
313.	人 気	c.	a public promise
314.	消 極	d.	human feeling
315.	世 話	e.	care
		f.	popularity

316.	衆 院	a.	bygone days
317.	更 迭	b.	trust
318.	過 去	c.	House of Councilors
319.	定 期	d.	periodical
320.	信 任	e.	a change
		f.	House of Representatives

321.	適 当	a.	closing
322.	打 合	b.	real ability
323.	閉 鎖	c.	arrangement
324.	削 減	d.	curtailment
325.	実 力	e.	adequate
		f.	fighting

326.	募 集	a.	disposition
327.	完 納	b.	backing
328.	払 下	c.	numeral
329.	応 援	d.	rejection
330.	数 字	e.	pay in full
		f.	recruiting

331.	否 定	a.	a session
332.	陳 情	b.	trade and commerce
333.	会 期	c.	business
334.	通 商	d.	negation
335.	公 民	e.	a citizen
		f.	petition

336.	収 穫	a.	benevolent
337.	卒 業	b.	crop
338.	中 間	c.	reciprocity
339.	互 恵	d.	a business
340.	営 業	e.	the middle
		f.	graduation

341.	回 復	a.	recovery
342.	主 要	b.	principal
		c.	a branch office
343.	支 局	d.	round about
344.	官 庁	e.	government offices
345.	進 出	f.	advance

346.	公 開	a.	a right
347.	気 象	b.	advantage
		c.	a sacrifice
348.	権 利	d.	weather
349.	達 成	e.	open to the public
350.	犠 牲	f.	attainment

351.	損 害	a.	physical education
352.	体 育	b.	damage
353.	累 増	c.	reality
		d.	continuous increase
354.	人 権	e.	failure
355.	現 実	f.	human rights

356.	減 少	a.	practice
357.	練 習	b.	fine arts
		c.	superficial
358.	美 術	d.	manifestation
359.	解 説	e.	a commentary
360.	表 明	f.	a decrease

361.	能 力	a.	an ability
362.	発 電	b.	finding employment
363.	経 費	c.	intelligent
		d.	limitation
364.	就 職	e.	expenses
365.	限 度	f.	generation of electricity

366.	中 継	a.	a hand rail
367.	出 発	b.	discretion
		c.	a means
368.	携 帯	d.	relay
369.	手 段	e.	departure
370.	慎 重	f.	portable

371.	発 展	a.	manufacturing
372.	統 計	b.	development
		c.	inside
373.	競 争	d.	statistics
374.	内 部	e.	unification
375.	製 作	f.	competition

376.	途 中	a.	en route
377.	野 菜	b.	factionalism
		c.	vegetables
378.	諮 問	d.	middle road
379.	奨 励	e.	an inquiry
380.	派 閥	f.	encouragement

381.	放 棄	a.	market price
382.	思 想	b.	a promise
		c.	thought
383.	約 束	d.	abandonment
384.	処 置	e.	a measure
385.	相 場	f.	meeting place

386.	直 後	a.	passing
387.	経 過	b.	liveliness
		c.	premier
388.	信 用	d.	credit
389.	総 理	e.	immediately after
390.	活 発	f.	progression

391.	賛 成	a.	a satellite
392.	指 摘	b.	guiding light
393.	処 分	c.	jury
394.	陪 審	d.	disposal
395.	衛 星	e.	point out
		f.	agree

396.	景 気	a.	a spear
397.	借 款	b.	amusement
398.	提 携	c.	cooperation
399.	矛 盾	d.	a loan
400.	娯 楽	e.	an economic boom
		f.	contradiction

◆ ANSWER SHEET ◆

	a	b	c	d	e	f
1 ···	□	□	□	□	□	□
2 ···	□	□	□	□	□	□
3 ···	□	□	□	□	□	□
4 ···	□	□	□	□	□	□
5 ···	□	□	□	□	□	□
6 ···	□	□	□	□	□	□
7 ···	□	□	□	□	□	□
8 ···	□	□	□	□	□	□
9 ···	□	□	□	□	□	□
10 ···	□	□	□	□	□	□
11 ···	□	□	□	□	□	□
12 ···	□	□	□	□	□	□
13 ···	□	□	□	□	□	□
14 ···	□	□	□	□	□	□
15 ···	□	□	□	□	□	□
16 ···	□	□	□	□	□	□
17 ···	□	□	□	□	□	□
18 ···	□	□	□	□	□	□
19 ···	□	□	□	□	□	□
20 ···	□	□	□	□	□	□

	a	b	c	d	e	f
21 ···	□	□	□	□	□	□
22 ···	□	□	□	□	□	□
23 ···	□	□	□	□	□	□
24 ···	□	□	□	□	□	□
25 ···	□	□	□	□	□	□
26 ···	□	□	□	□	□	□
27 ···	□	□	□	□	□	□
28 ···	□	□	□	□	□	□
29 ···	□	□	□	□	□	□
30 ···	□	□	□	□	□	□
31 ···	□	□	□	□	□	□
32 ···	□	□	□	□	□	□
33 ···	□	□	□	□	□	□
34 ···	□	□	□	□	□	□
35 ···	□	□	□	□	□	□
36 ···	□	□	□	□	□	□
37 ···	□	□	□	□	□	□
38 ···	□	□	□	□	□	□
39 ···	□	□	□	□	□	□
40 ···	□	□	□	□	□	□

	a	b	c	d	e	f		a	b	c	d	e	f
41 ···	☐	☐	☐	☐	☐	☐	67 ···	☐	☐	☐	☐	☐	☐
42 ···	☐	☐	☐	☐	☐	☐	68 ···	☐	☐	☐	☐	☐	☐
43 ···	☐	☐	☐	☐	☐	☐	69 ···	☐	☐	☐	☐	☐	☐
44 ···	☐	☐	☐	☐	☐	☐	70 ···	☐	☐	☐	☐	☐	☐
45 ···	☐	☐	☐	☐	☐	☐	71 ···	☐	☐	☐	☐	☐	☐
46 ···	☐	☐	☐	☐	☐	☐	72 ···	☐	☐	☐	☐	☐	☐
47 ···	☐	☐	☐	☐	☐	☐	73 ···	☐	☐	☐	☐	☐	☐
48 ···	☐	☐	☐	☐	☐	☐	74 ···	☐	☐	☐	☐	☐	☐
49 ···	☐	☐	☐	☐	☐	☐	75 ···	☐	☐	☐	☐	☐	☐
50 ···	☐	☐	☐	☐	☐	☐	76 ···	☐	☐	☐	☐	☐	☐
51 ···	☐	☐	☐	☐	☐	☐	77 ···	☐	☐	☐	☐	☐	☐
52 ···	☐	☐	☐	☐	☐	☐	78 ···	☐	☐	☐	☐	☐	☐
53 ···	☐	☐	☐	☐	☐	☐	79 ···	☐	☐	☐	☐	☐	☐
54 ···	☐	☐	☐	☐	☐	☐	80 ···	☐	☐	☐	☐	☐	☐
55 ···	☐	☐	☐	☐	☐	☐	81 ···	☐	☐	☐	☐	☐	☐
56 ···	☐	☐	☐	☐	☐	☐	82 ···	☐	☐	☐	☐	☐	☐
57 ···	☐	☐	☐	☐	☐	☐	83 ···	☐	☐	☐	☐	☐	☐
58 ···	☐	☐	☐	☐	☐	☐	84 ···	☐	☐	☐	☐	☐	☐
59 ···	☐	☐	☐	☐	☐	☐	85 ···	☐	☐	☐	☐	☐	☐
60 ···	☐	☐	☐	☐	☐	☐	86 ···	☐	☐	☐	☐	☐	☐
61 ···	☐	☐	☐	☐	☐	☐	87 ···	☐	☐	☐	☐	☐	☐
62 ···	☐	☐	☐	☐	☐	☐	88 ···	☐	☐	☐	☐	☐	☐
63 ···	☐	☐	☐	☐	☐	☐	89 ···	☐	☐	☐	☐	☐	☐
64 ···	☐	☐	☐	☐	☐	☐	90 ···	☐	☐	☐	☐	☐	☐
65 ···	☐	☐	☐	☐	☐	☐	91 ···	☐	☐	☐	☐	☐	☐
66 ···	☐	☐	☐	☐	☐	☐	92 ···	☐	☐	☐	☐	☐	☐

	a	b	c	d	e	f		a	b	c	d	e	f
93 …	□	□	□	□	□	□	119 …	□	□	□	□	□	□
94 …	□	□	□	□	□	□	120 …	□	□	□	□	□	□
95 …	□	□	□	□	□	□	121 …	□	□	□	□	□	□
96 …	□	□	□	□	□	□	122 …	□	□	□	□	□	□
97 …	□	□	□	□	□	□	123 …	□	□	□	□	□	□
98 …	□	□	□	□	□	□	124 …	□	□	□	□	□	□
99 …	□	□	□	□	□	□	125 …	□	□	□	□	□	□
100 …	□	□	□	□	□	□	126 …	□	□	□	□	□	□
101 …	□	□	□	□	□	□	127 …	□	□	□	□	□	□
102 …	□	□	□	□	□	□	128 …	□	□	□	□	□	□
103 …	□	□	□	□	□	□	129 …	□	□	□	□	□	□
104 …	□	□	□	□	□	□	130 …	□	□	□	□	□	□
105 …	□	□	□	□	□	□	131 …	□	□	□	□	□	□
106 …	□	□	□	□	□	□	132 …	□	□	□	□	□	□
107 …	□	□	□	□	□	□	133 …	□	□	□	□	□	□
108 …	□	□	□	□	□	□	134 …	□	□	□	□	□	□
109 …	□	□	□	□	□	□	135 …	□	□	□	□	□	□
110 …	□	□	□	□	□	□	136 …	□	□	□	□	□	□
111 …	□	□	□	□	□	□	137 …	□	□	□	□	□	□
112 …	□	□	□	□	□	□	138 …	□	□	□	□	□	□
113 …	□	□	□	□	□	□	139 …	□	□	□	□	□	□
114 …	□	□	□	□	□	□	140 …	□	□	□	□	□	□
115 …	□	□	□	□	□	□	141 …	□	□	□	□	□	□
116 …	□	□	□	□	□	□	142 …	□	□	□	□	□	□
117 …	□	□	□	□	□	□	143 …	□	□	□	□	□	□
118 …	□	□	□	□	□	□	144 …	□	□	□	□	□	□

	a	b	c	d	e	f			a	b	c	d	e	f
145 ···	□	□	□	□	□	□		171 ···	□	□	□	□	□	□
146 ···	□	□	□	□	□	□		172 ···	□	□	□	□	□	□
147 ···	□	□	□	□	□	□		173 ···	□	□	□	□	□	□
148 ···	□	□	□	□	□	□		174 ···	□	□	□	□	□	□
149 ···	□	□	□	□	□	□		175 ···	□	□	□	□	□	□
150 ···	□	□	□	□	□	□		176 ···	□	□	□	□	□	□
151 ···	□	□	□	□	□	□		177 ···	□	□	□	□	□	□
152 ···	□	□	□	□	□	□		178 ···	□	□	□	□	□	□
153 ···	□	□	□	□	□	□		179 ···	□	□	□	□	□	□
154 ···	□	□	□	□	□	□		180 ···	□	□	□	□	□	□
155 ···	□	□	□	□	□	□		181 ···	□	□	□	□	□	□
156 ···	□	□	□	□	□	□		182 ···	□	□	□	□	□	□
157 ···	□	□	□	□	□	□		183 ···	□	□	□	□	□	□
158 ···	□	□	□	□	□	□		184 ···	□	□	□	□	□	□
159 ···	□	□	□	□	□	□		185 ···	□	□	□	□	□	□
160 ···	□	□	□	□	□	□		186 ···	□	□	□	□	□	□
161 ···	□	□	□	□	□	□		187 ···	□	□	□	□	□	□
162 ···	□	□	□	□	□	□		188 ···	□	□	□	□	□	□
163 ···	□	□	□	□	□	□		189 ···	□	□	□	□	□	□
164 ···	□	□	□	□	□	□		190 ···	□	□	□	□	□	□
165 ···	□	□	□	□	□	□		191 ···	□	□	□	□	□	□
166 ···	□	□	□	□	□	□		192 ···	□	□	□	□	□	□
167 ···	□	□	□	□	□	□		193 ···	□	□	□	□	□	□
168 ···	□	□	□	□	□	□		194 ···	□	□	□	□	□	□
169 ···	□	□	□	□	□	□		195 ···	□	□	□	□	□	□
170 ···	□	□	□	□	□	□		196 ···	□	□	□	□	□	□

	a	b	c	d	e	f		a	b	c	d	e	f
197 …	□	□	□	□	□	□	223 …	□	□	□	□	□	□
198 …	□	□	□	□	□	□	224 …	□	□	□	□	□	□
199 …	□	□	□	□	□	□	225 …	□	□	□	□	□	□
200 …	□	□	□	□	□	□	226 …	□	□	□	□	□	□
201 …	□	□	□	□	□	□	227 …	□	□	□	□	□	□
202 …	□	□	□	□	□	□	228 …	□	□	□	□	□	□
203 …	□	□	□	□	□	□	229 …	□	□	□	□	□	□
204 …	□	□	□	□	□	□	230 …	□	□	□	□	□	□
205 …	□	□	□	□	□	□	231 …	□	□	□	□	□	□
206 …	□	□	□	□	□	□	232 …	□	□	□	□	□	□
207 …	□	□	□	□	□	□	233 …	□	□	□	□	□	□
208 …	□	□	□	□	□	□	234 …	□	□	□	□	□	□
209 …	□	□	□	□	□	□	235 …	□	□	□	□	□	□
210 …	□	□	□	□	□	□	236 …	□	□	□	□	□	□
211 …	□	□	□	□	□	□	237 …	□	□	□	□	□	□
212 …	□	□	□	□	□	□	238 …	□	□	□	□	□	□
213 …	□	□	□	□	□	□	239 …	□	□	□	□	□	□
214 …	□	□	□	□	□	□	240 …	□	□	□	□	□	□
215 …	□	□	□	□	□	□	241 …	□	□	□	□	□	□
216 …	□	□	□	□	□	□	242 …	□	□	□	□	□	□
217 …	□	□	□	□	□	□	243 …	□	□	□	□	□	□
218 …	□	□	□	□	□	□	244 …	□	□	□	□	□	□
219 …	□	□	□	□	□	□	245 …	□	□	□	□	□	□
220 …	□	□	□	□	□	□	246 …	□	□	□	□	□	□
221 …	□	□	□	□	□	□	247 …	□	□	□	□	□	□
222 …	□	□	□	□	□	□	248 …	□	□	□	□	□	□

	a	b	c	d	e	f		a	b	c	d	e	f
249 ⋯	□	□	□	□	□	□	275 ⋯	□	□	□	□	□	□
250 ⋯	□	□	□	□	□	□	276 ⋯	□	□	□	□	□	□
251 ⋯	□	□	□	□	□	□	277 ⋯	□	□	□	□	□	□
252 ⋯	□	□	□	□	□	□	278 ⋯	□	□	□	□	□	□
253 ⋯	□	□	□	□	□	□	279 ⋯	□	□	□	□	□	□
254 ⋯	□	□	□	□	□	□	280 ⋯	□	□	□	□	□	□
255 ⋯	□	□	□	□	□	□	281 ⋯	□	□	□	□	□	□
256 ⋯	□	□	□	□	□	□	282 ⋯	□	□	□	□	□	□
257 ⋯	□	□	□	□	□	□	283 ⋯	□	□	□	□	□	□
258 ⋯	□	□	□	□	□	□	284 ⋯	□	□	□	□	□	□
259 ⋯	□	□	□	□	□	□	285 ⋯	□	□	□	□	□	□
260 ⋯	□	□	□	□	□	□	286 ⋯	□	□	□	□	□	□
261 ⋯	□	□	□	□	□	□	287 ⋯	□	□	□	□	□	□
262 ⋯	□	□	□	□	□	□	288 ⋯	□	□	□	□	□	□
263 ⋯	□	□	□	□	□	□	289 ⋯	□	□	□	□	□	□
264 ⋯	□	□	□	□	□	□	290 ⋯	□	□	□	□	□	□
265 ⋯	□	□	□	□	□	□	291 ⋯	□	□	□	□	□	□
266 ⋯	□	□	□	□	□	□	292 ⋯	□	□	□	□	□	□
267 ⋯	□	□	□	□	□	□	293 ⋯	□	□	□	□	□	□
268 ⋯	□	□	□	□	□	□	294 ⋯	□	□	□	□	□	□
269 ⋯	□	□	□	□	□	□	295 ⋯	□	□	□	□	□	□
270 ⋯	□	□	□	□	□	□	296 ⋯	□	□	□	□	□	□
271 ⋯	□	□	□	□	□	□	297 ⋯	□	□	□	□	□	□
272 ⋯	□	□	□	□	□	□	298 ⋯	□	□	□	□	□	□
273 ⋯	□	□	□	□	□	□	299 ⋯	□	□	□	□	□	□
274 ⋯	□	□	□	□	□	□	300 ⋯	□	□	□	□	□	□

	a	b	c	d	e	f		a	b	c	d	e	f
301 …	☐	☐	☐	☐	☐	☐	327 …	☐	☐	☐	☐	☐	☐
302 …	☐	☐	☐	☐	☐	☐	328 …	☐	☐	☐	☐	☐	☐
303 …	☐	☐	☐	☐	☐	☐	329 …	☐	☐	☐	☐	☐	☐
304 …	☐	☐	☐	☐	☐	☐	330 …	☐	☐	☐	☐	☐	☐
305 …	☐	☐	☐	☐	☐	☐	331 …	☐	☐	☐	☐	☐	☐
306 …	☐	☐	☐	☐	☐	☐	332 …	☐	☐	☐	☐	☐	☐
307 …	☐	☐	☐	☐	☐	☐	333 …	☐	☐	☐	☐	☐	☐
308 …	☐	☐	☐	☐	☐	☐	334 …	☐	☐	☐	☐	☐	☐
309 …	☐	☐	☐	☐	☐	☐	335 …	☐	☐	☐	☐	☐	☐
310 …	☐	☐	☐	☐	☐	☐	336 …	☐	☐	☐	☐	☐	☐
311 …	☐	☐	☐	☐	☐	☐	337 …	☐	☐	☐	☐	☐	☐
312 …	☐	☐	☐	☐	☐	☐	338 …	☐	☐	☐	☐	☐	☐
313 …	☐	☐	☐	☐	☐	☐	339 …	☐	☐	☐	☐	☐	☐
314 …	☐	☐	☐	☐	☐	☐	340 …	☐	☐	☐	☐	☐	☐
315 …	☐	☐	☐	☐	☐	☐	341 …	☐	☐	☐	☐	☐	☐
316 …	☐	☐	☐	☐	☐	☐	342 …	☐	☐	☐	☐	☐	☐
317 …	☐	☐	☐	☐	☐	☐	343 …	☐	☐	☐	☐	☐	☐
318 …	☐	☐	☐	☐	☐	☐	344 …	☐	☐	☐	☐	☐	☐
319 …	☐	☐	☐	☐	☐	☐	345 …	☐	☐	☐	☐	☐	☐
320 …	☐	☐	☐	☐	☐	☐	346 …	☐	☐	☐	☐	☐	☐
321 …	☐	☐	☐	☐	☐	☐	347 …	☐	☐	☐	☐	☐	☐
322 …	☐	☐	☐	☐	☐	☐	348 …	☐	☐	☐	☐	☐	☐
323 …	☐	☐	☐	☐	☐	☐	349 …	☐	☐	☐	☐	☐	☐
324 …	☐	☐	☐	☐	☐	☐	350 …	☐	☐	☐	☐	☐	☐
325 …	☐	☐	☐	☐	☐	☐	351 …	☐	☐	☐	☐	☐	☐
326 …	☐	☐	☐	☐	☐	☐	352 …	☐	☐	☐	☐	☐	☐

	a	b	c	d	e	f			a	b	c	d	e	f
353 ···	□	□	□	□	□	□	377 ···	□	□	□	□	□	□
354 ···	□	□	□	□	□	□	378 ···	□	□	□	□	□	□
355 ···	□	□	□	□	□	□	379 ···	□	□	□	□	□	□
356 ···	□	□	□	□	□	□	380 ···	□	□	□	□	□	□
357 ···	□	□	□	□	□	□	381 ···	□	□	□	□	□	□
358 ···	□	□	□	□	□	□	382 ···	□	□	□	□	□	□
359 ···	□	□	□	□	□	□	383 ···	□	□	□	□	□	□
360 ···	□	□	□	□	□	□	384 ···	□	□	□	□	□	□
361 ···	□	□	□	□	□	□	385 ···	□	□	□	□	□	□
362 ···	□	□	□	□	□	□	386 ···	□	□	□	□	□	□
363 ···	□	□	□	□	□	□	387 ···	□	□	□	□	□	□
364 ···	□	□	□	□	□	□	388 ···	□	□	□	□	□	□
365 ···	□	□	□	□	□	□	389 ···	□	□	□	□	□	□
366 ···	□	□	□	□	□	□	390 ···	□	□	□	□	□	□
367 ···	□	□	□	□	□	□	391 ···	□	□	□	□	□	□
368 ···	□	□	□	□	□	□	392 ···	□	□	□	□	□	□
369 ···	□	□	□	□	□	□	393 ···	□	□	□	□	□	□
370 ···	□	□	□	□	□	□	394 ···	□	□	□	□	□	□
371 ···	□	□	□	□	□	□	395 ···	□	□	□	□	□	□
372 ···	□	□	□	□	□	□	396 ···	□	□	□	□	□	□
373 ···	□	□	□	□	□	□	397 ···	□	□	□	□	□	□
374 ···	□	□	□	□	□	□	398 ···	□	□	□	□	□	□
375 ···	□	□	□	□	□	□	399 ···	□	□	□	□	□	□
376 ···	□	□	□	□	□	□	400 ···	□	□	□	□	□	□

◆ INDEX ◆

Numbers correspond to those in the list of character compounds.

◆ ANSWERS TO TEST ◆

1 – f	32 – a	63 – e	94 – c
2 – d	33 – b	64 – c	95 – a
3 – c	34 – d	65 – b	96 – c
4 – b	35 – e	66 – b	97 – d
5 – a	36 – c	67 – d	98 – b
6 – f	37 – d	68 – e	99 – a
7 – e	38 – b	69 – f	100 – e
8 – a	39 – a	70 – a	101 – c
9 – b	40 – e	71 – e	102 – e
10 – c	41 – d	72 – a	103 – f
11 – f	42 – a	73 – b	104 – a
12 – e	43 – f	74 – f	105 – d
13 – a	44 – b	75 – c	106 – f
14 – b	45 – c	76 – e	107 – c
15 – c	46 – c	77 – f	108 – b
16 – f	47 – a	78 – a	109 – d
17 – e	48 – b	79 – b	110 – a
18 – a	49 – f	80 – d	111 – b
19 – b	50 – d	81 – c	112 – f
20 – c	51 – c	82 – e	113 – d
21 – e	52 – a	83 – a	114 – a
22 – a	53 – f	84 – b	115 – c
23 – b	54 – b	85 – f	116 – c
24 – c	55 – d	86 – c	117 – d
25 – d	56 – c	87 – f	118 – e
26 – c	57 – a	88 – b	119 – f
27 – f	58 – b	89 – a	120 – b
28 – a	59 – f	90 – d	121 – b
29 – b	60 – d	91 – b	122 – a
30 – d	61 – d	92 – f	123 – d
31 – c	62 – f	93 – d	124 – e

125 – c	163 – a	201 – d	239 – e
126 – c	164 – c	202 – f	240 – f
127 – a	165 – d	203 – c	241 – b
128 – b	166 – f	204 – b	242 – d
129 – d	167 – a	205 – a	243 – c
130 – e	168 – e	206 – a	244 – f
131 – c	169 – b	207 – b	245 – a
132 – d	170 – c	208 – e	246 – e
133 – a	171 – e	209 – f	247 – f
134 – e	172 – a	210 – d	248 – d
135 – f	173 – d	211 – d	249 – c
136 – c	174 – b	212 – e	250 – b
137 – e	175 – f	213 – c	251 – a
138 – f	176 – d	214 – f	252 – b
139 – a	177 – a	215 – b	253 – d
140 – b	178 – f	216 – a	254 – c
141 – c	179 – c	217 – d	255 – e
142 – d	180 – b	218 – b	256 – b
143 – e	181 – e	219 – f	257 – d
144 – b	182 – d	220 – e	258 – a
145 – f	183 – a	221 – f	259 – c
146 – c	184 – f	222 – e	260 – f
147 – f	185 – c	223 – c	261 – e
148 – b	186 – b	224 – b	262 – a
149 – a	187 – d	225 – a	263 – b
150 – d	188 – f	226 – d	264 – c
151 – d	189 – c	227 – c	265 – f
152 – e	190 – a	228 – f	266 – e
153 – a	191 – c	229 – b	267 – f
154 – c	192 – d	230 – a	268 – c
155 – b	193 – e	231 – a	269 – d
156 – f	194 – f	232 – c	270 – b
157 – a	195 – a	233 – b	271 – c
158 – c	196 – b	234 – d	272 – d
159 – e	197 – c	235 – e	273 – e
160 – b	198 – d	236 – d	274 – f
161 – f	199 – f	237 – a	275 – a
162 – e	200 – a	238 – c	276 – a

277 – b	308 – d	339 – c	370 – b
278 – d	309 – f	340 – d	371 – b
279 – e	310 – e	341 – a	372 – d
280 – c	311 – a	342 – b	373 – f
281 – d	312 – c	343 – c	374 – c
282 – e	313 – f	344 – e	375 – a
283 – c	314 – b	345 – f	376 – a
284 – f	315 – e	346 – e	377 – c
285 – b	316 – f	347 – d	378 – e
286 – a	317 – e	348 – a	379 – f
287 – c	318 – a	349 – f	380 – b
288 – b	319 – d	350 – c	381 – d
289 – d	320 – b	351 – b	382 – c
290 – e	321 – e	352 – a	383 – b
291 – c	322 – c	353 – d	384 – e
292 – b	323 – a	354 – f	385 – a
293 – a	324 – d	355 – c	386 – e
294 – d	325 – b	356 – f	387 – a
295 – f	326 – f	357 – a	388 – d
296 – a	327 – e	358 – b	389 – c
297 – d	328 – a	359 – e	390 – b
298 – c	329 – b	360 – d	391 – f
299 – b	330 – c	361 – a	392 – e
300 – f	331 – d	362 – f	393 – d
301 – c	332 – f	363 – e	394 – c
302 – d	333 – a	364 – b	395 – a
303 – b	334 – b	365 – d	396 – e
304 – f	335 – e	366 – d	397 – d
305 – e	336 – b	367 – e	398 – c
306 – a	337 – f	368 – f	399 – f
307 – c	338 – e	369 – c	400 – b